Bonds, Preferred Stocks, and the Money Market

The Basic Investor's Library

Alternative Investments

Bonds, Preferred Stocks, and the Money Market

Careers in the Investment World

Growth Stocks

Investing and Trading

Investment Banking

Investments and the Law

Mutual Funds

Reading the Financial Pages

Stock Options

The Principles of Technical Analysis

Understanding A Company

Wall Street—How It Works

What Is a Share of Stock?

Chelsea House Publishers

Bonds, Preferred Stocks, and the Money Market

JEFFREY B. LITTLE

Paul A. Samuelson
Senior Editorial Consultant

CHELSEA HOUSE PUBLISHERS New York Philadelphia

Editor-in-Chief Nancy Toff
Executive Editor Remmel T. Nunn
Managing Editor Karyn Gullen Browne
Copy Chief Juliann Barbato
Picture Editor Adrian G. Allen
Art Director Giannella Garrett
Manufacturing Manager Gerald Levine

Staff for BONDS, PREFERRED STOCKS, AND THE MONEY MARKET
Senior Editor Marjorie P. K. Weiser
Associate Editor Andrea E. Reynolds
Assistant Editor Karen Schimmel
Copyeditor James Guiry
Deputy Copy Chief Ellen Scordato
Editorial Assistant Tara P. Deal
Associate Picture Editor Juliette Dickstein
Picture Researcher Betsy Levin
Senior Designer Laurie Jewell
Designer Ghila Krajzman
Production Coordinator Joseph Romano

Contributing Editor Pat Dreyfus
Consulting Editor Shawn Patrick Burke

Copyright © 1988 by Chelsea House Publishers, a division of Main Line Book Co. All rights reserved. Printed and bound in the United States of America.

3 5 7 9 8 6 4 2

Library of Congress Cataloging in Publication Data

Little, Jeffrey B.
  Bonds, preferred stocks, and the money market / Jeffrey B. Little.
    p. cm.—(The Basic investor's library)
  Bibliography: p.
  Includes index.
  Summary: Explains investment alternatives to common stocks, specifically bonds, preferred stocks, and money market instruments.
  ISBN 1-55546-625-7
    0-7910-0311-6 (pbk.)

  1. Bonds—Juvenile literature. 2. Preferred stocks—Juvenile literature. 3. Money market funds—Juvenile literature.
[1. Bonds. 2. Stocks. 3. Money market.] I. Title. II. Series.
HG4651.L57 1988
332.63'225—dc19   87-30277
                                                      CIP
                                                       AC

CONTENTS

Foreword: Learning the Tools of Investing
   by Paul A. Samuelson _____ 6

Bonds, Preferred Stocks, and the Money Market _____ 9

Bonds _____ 10
   U.S. Government Securities _____ 25
   Agency Issues _____ 27
   Corporate Bonds _____ 29
   Municipal Bonds _____ 31
   Convertible Bonds _____ 34

Getting Started in Bonds _____ 36

Preferred Stocks _____ 37

The Money Market _____ 40

Glossary _____ 44

Further Reading _____ 46

Index _____ 46

Learning the Tools of Investing

PAUL A. SAMUELSON

When asked why the great financial house of Morgan had been so successful, J. Pierpont Morgan replied, "Do you suppose that's because we take money seriously?"

Managing our personal finances is a serious business, and something we all must learn to do. We begin life dependent on someone else's income and capital. But after we become independent, it is a remorseless fact of nature that we must not only support ourselves for the present but must also start saving money for retirement. The best theory of saving that economists have is built upon this model of *life-cycle saving*: You must provide in the long years of prime working life for what modern medicine has lengthened to, potentially, decades of retirement. This life-cycle model won a 1985 Nobel Prize for my MIT colleague Franco Modigliani, and it points up the need to learn the rudiments of personal finance.

Learning to acquire wealth, however, is only part of the story. We must also learn to avoid losing what we have acquired. There is an old saying that "life insurance is *sold*, not bought." The same goes for stocks and bonds. In each case, the broker is guaranteed a profit, whether or not the customer benefits from the transaction. Knowledge is the customer's only true ally in the world of finance. Some gullible victims have lost their lifetime savings to unscrupulous sales promoters. One chap buys the Brooklyn Bridge. Another believes a stranger who asserts that gold will quickly double in price, with no risk of a drop in value. Such "con" (confidence) rackets get written up in the newspapers and on the police blotters every day.

I am concerned, however, about something less dramatic than con artists; something that is not at all illegal, but that costs ordinary citizens a thousand times more than outright embezzlement or fraud. Consider two families, neighbors who could be found in any town. They started alike. Each worked equally hard, and had about the same income. But the Smiths have to make do with half of what the Joneses have in retirement income, for one simple reason: The Joneses followed prudent practice as savers and investors, while the Smiths tried to make a killing and constantly bought and sold stocks at high commissions.

The point is, it does matter to learn how financial markets work, and how you can participate in them to your best advantage. It is important to know the difference between *common* and *preferred* stocks, between *convertible* and *zero-coupon* bonds. It is not difficult to find out what *mutual funds* are, and to understand the difference between the successful Fund A, which charges no commission, or "load," and the equally successful Fund B, which does charge the buyer such a fee.

All investing involves risk. When I was a young assistant professor, I said primly to my great Harvard teacher, Joseph Schumpeter: "We should speculate only with money we can afford to lose." He gently corrected me: "Paul, there is no such money. Besides, a speculator is merely an investor who has lost." Did Schumpeter exaggerate? Of course he did, but in the good cause of establishing the basic point of financial management: Good past performance is no guarantee of the future.

That is why *diversification* is the golden rule. "Don't put all your eggs in one basket. And watch all those baskets!" However, diversification does not mean throwing random darts at the financial pages of the newspaper to choose the best stocks in which to invest. The most diversified strategy of all would be to invest in a portfolio containing all the stocks in the comprehensive Standard & Poor's 500 Stock Index. But rather than throw random darts at the financial pages to pick out a few stocks, why not throw a large bath towel at the newspaper instead? Buy a bit of everything in proportion to its value in the larger world: Buy more General Motors than Ford, because GM is the bigger company; buy General Electric as well as GM because the auto industry is just one of many industries. That is called being an *index investor*. Index investing makes sense because 70 out of 100 investors who try to do better than the Standard & Poor's 500, the sober record shows, do worse over a 30-year period.

Do not take my word for this. The second lesson in finance is to be skeptical of what writers and other experts say, and that includes being skeptical of professors of economics. So I wish readers *Bon voyage!* on their cruise to command the fundamentals of investing. On your mainship flag, replace the motto "Nothing ventured, nothing gained" with the Latin words *Caveat emptor*—Let the buyer beware.

Bonds, Preferred Stocks, and the Money Market

Most investors put their money in common stocks or in stock mutual funds. They have heard something about bonds, and perhaps other investment possibilities, but dismiss these as being too complex for them, or only for those who have a fortune available for "playing the market." However, the alternatives to investing in common stocks are many and not all that difficult to understand. Wise investors tailor their portfolios, or group of investments, to fit their financial situations. They change their portfolios periodically as their financial needs change over time.

This book presents some of the alternatives to common stocks that should be considered in a lifetime of changing financial needs and investment objectives—bonds, convertible securities, preferred stocks, and money market investments. It also shows how some of these alternatives can have a place in an average investor's portfolio, especially for those who require more current income and greater safety of principal than can be expected of a portfolio invested entirely in common stocks.

Many people become bondholders at an early age. U.S. Government savings bonds are popular gifts for births, christenings, and other special occasions.

BONDS

In the view of many people, bonds are also-rans, less glamorous and interesting than stocks. Television and radio news reports frequently conclude with a description of the day's stock market activity, but there is seldom, if ever, any mention of bonds. Some commonly held opinions are that "bonds are just for the rich," "bonds are strictly for retirement," and "bonds are a conservative investment."

Let us examine these notions. First: "Bonds are for the rich." You probably do not think of yourself as rich, but you may well be a bondholder. Did you, like many Americans, receive $25 or $50 savings bonds when you were born or to celebrate some other occasion? Most bonds cost $1,000 or less, although they can also be bought in larger denominations.

Second: "Bonds are for retirement" or the elderly. It is true that as people grow older they usually want reliable income from their investments. But financial advisors recommend that every portfolio should include some interest-bearing securities to provide predictable income. Such experts often advise that people who are just starting to earn and invest should concentrate on common stocks but have 10 to 15 percent of their investment money in a short-term account, such as a money market fund, and another 20 to 25 percent in bonds. These percentages will later change according to general economic conditions and the individual's personal circumstances.

Third: "Bonds are a conservative investment." This may have been true for decades, but in the 1970s double-digit inflation and skyrocketing interest rates knocked bond prices for a loop. As the purchasing power of the dollar declined by more than 10 percent a year, interest rates rose to 15 percent and more. Bonds were no longer as reliable or stable as people had always thought. More recently, bond prices can fluctuate as much in a day as they once did in a year. Many sophisticated investors, and certainly institutional investors (who have huge sums of money to invest for large organizations), buy bonds not so much for interest income as in the hope of making a profit from future price rises. Now that we have cleared up a few myths about bonds, let us look at how they work and how you as a potential investor can use them.

What Is a Bond?

A bond represents a loan, made by the bond buyer to the organization that issued (created) the bond. Like the contract you must sign if you take out a bank loan, a bond is a formal IOU. The organizations that issue bonds are corporations and federal, state, and local governments and their agencies. Each type of bond is known to investment professionals by a single word: "corporates," "governments," "municipals," and "agencies."

The issuing organization promises to pay bond buyers a fixed rate of interest, usually in semiannual installments, and to repay the loan in full by a specified date. In most cases a bond's only backing is the full faith and credit of

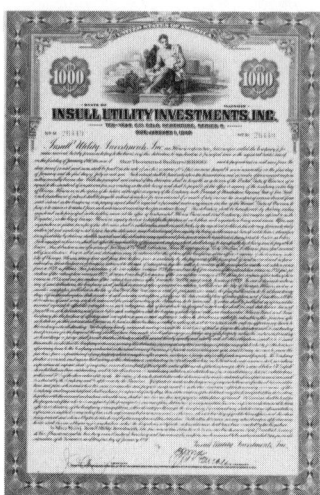

Bonds represent corporate or government debt. The borrower issues a certificate similar to this one, which states the terms of the loan made by the bond buyer: the face value of the bond, the rate, and the maturity date at which the loan is to be repaid in full. Until 1983, coupons like those at the right were usually attached to bonds. To receive each semiannual interest payment, bondholders had to turn in the appropriate coupon. This method is no longer used, but the interest rate on a bond is still called its coupon.

the borrowing organization, which is why U.S. government bonds or *obligations* rank highest for safety. Sometimes a less reliable borrower will reinforce these promises by pledging *collateral*, such as equipment or property, to be claimed by the lender/buyer if the borrower cannot repay the loan on schedule.

Everything a lender/buyer needs to know can be learned by reading the information printed on the face, or front, of a bond. Here you will find the amount to be repaid, known as the *principal, par value,* or *face value*. The *maturity date*, when the issuer must repay the principal, tells you the bond's *term*, or life expectancy. The interest rate is called the *coupon*, a holdover from the days when nearly all bonds came with coupons attached. On each coupon was printed a date on which the bond issuer had to pay interest. Bondholders clipped these coupons on those dates and sent the coupons to the bond issuer for payment.

New kinds of fixed-income securities, introduced in the early 1980s, offer variations on the "plain-vanilla," or standard, bonds. These were designed to attract additional investors. *Zero-coupon bonds,* or "zeros," sell for a fraction of their face value and pay no interest until they mature. *Put bonds* entitle investors to sell (put) their bonds back to the issuer on one or more specified dates. Investors receive full face value for each bond, even though the market price of the issue may be lower than when they bought it. The issuers of *floating-rate bonds* adjust their yields periodically to bring them into line with prevailing interest rates.

Today, the names of all bond buyers are registered, meaning that they are on record with the corporation or institution that issued the securities. Before July 1983, however, the names of bond buyers, especially of municipals, were usually not registered with the issuing organization. With such *bearer bonds,* possession is 100 percent of the law: Whoever actually has them is presumed to own them.

The owner of a bond (or of a share of preferred stock, which we discuss on page 37) has rights different from the owner of a share of common stock. Common stockholders of a publicly traded company that prospers can expect to share in the expanding profits. They will benefit from both high dividends and rising stock prices. Corporate bondholders get little or no benefit from such growth, but they have a big advantage if the company fares poorly: They must be paid in full before common and preferred stockholders get as much as a penny. Because bonds and preferred stock give investors first call on an issuer's assets, they are known as *senior securities*.

Interest Rates and Bond Prices

The movement up or down of interest rates is the engine that drives bond prices. Think of this engine as operating a seesaw: When interest rates rise, bond prices fall. There is, then, an inverse relationship between interest rates and bond prices: As rates drop, prices climb. Although bond prices normally do not swing as widely as prices of common stocks, a bond may sell before its maturity date for more or less than the previous buyer paid for it. Investors are often willing to pay more than a bond's face value to snare an above-average yield when other interest rates are declining.

Interest is the "rent" paid for the use of money. This rent rises when there is heavy demand (many borrowers) and a limited supply of money. Light demand brings interest rates down.

The Federal Reserve Building in Washington, D.C., headquarters of the Federal Reserve Board, which supervises the banking system in the United States.

If bond prices vary inversely with interest rates, what is it that causes interest to fluctuate? Economic activity is one of the strongest influences on the direction of interest rates. During periods of economic expansion, corporations, governments, and individuals are all seeking to borrow money to finance their growth and development. The increase in demand causes rates to rise. Federal monetary policy is another powerful force. The Federal Reserve Board (the agency that supervises banking in the United States) can push rates up or down by raising or lowering the interest rate that banks within the Federal Reserve System must pay to borrow from one of the regional Federal Reserve Banks.

Investors' expectations of future interest rate patterns also affect rate levels. After a period of inflation (rising prices and lower purchasing power of money), for example, rates tend to stay high for a while, even after demand has eased. Lenders demand more "rent" to protect themselves, lest another round of rising interest rates and falling bond prices leave them with less money. A longer bond term leaves more room for something to go wrong. Buyers of bonds with distant maturity dates are compensated for uncertainty about the future by receiving higher interest rates than those offered people who buy short or intermediate term issues.

Which Rate Really Rates Several different but interrelated interest rates determine how much bond issuers must pay for the use of money. The *discount rate* is what member banks of the Federal Reserve System pay on funds borrowed from the Federal Reserve Bank. When one Federal Reserve member bank lends money to another, the borrower pays interest at the *federal funds rate*. When banks make loans to their most creditworthy (favored or prime) customers, usually corporations, they charge inter-

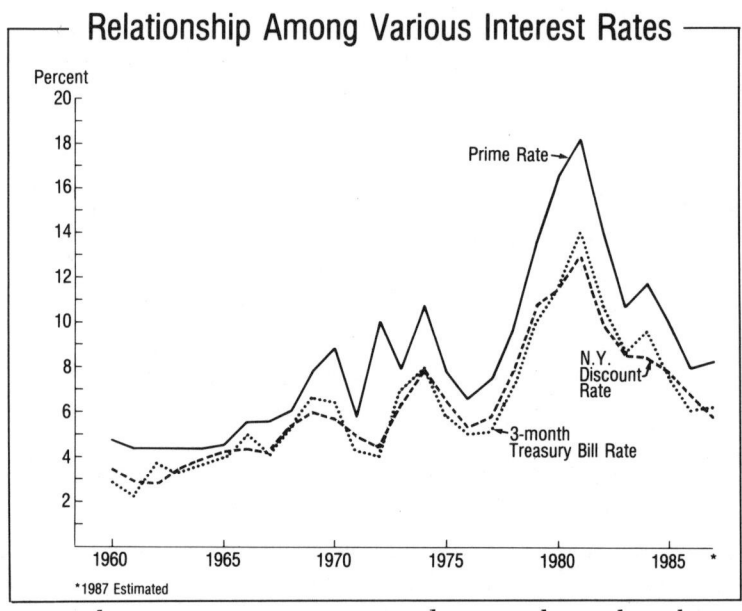

est at the *prime rate*. *Money market rates* hinge largely on the yield of three-month Treasury bills. Despite frequent differences of several percentage points between the various interest rates, all tend to move up or down together. (See graph above.)

Understanding Price Quotations   Most bonds are issued with face values of $1,000 or $5,000. When bonds are sold, their prices are listed in brokers' reports and the financial pages of newspapers. On the open market, a bond price is listed at one-tenth of its actual dollar value. Thus a bond selling for $100 above par (above face, or par, value), or $1,100, would be listed at 110. The amount above par is called the *premium*. A bond that sells below par is said to trade at a *discount*. Bonds, like stocks, trade at fractional prices in increments of eighths (eighths of $10; thus, ⅛ = $1.25). A bond priced at 88⅛ corresponds to a dollar value of $881.25, and one at 105⅞ sells for $1,058.75.

Government bonds are listed similarly, but fractions are expressed in thirty-seconds. One thirty-second of $10 is approximately 32 cents. A bond listing of 90.12 translates into 90 12/32 or 90 3/8, for a dollar equivalent of $903.75.

Shown below is a typical excerpt from the New York Exchange corporate bond table that appears daily in the financial pages of the *Wall Street Journal* and other newspapers. Locate the listing for a bond issued by the Exxon Corporation, a well-known oil company, paying annual interest of 6½ percent and maturing in 1998. On the day before this list was printed, the bond had a current yield of 8.6 percent. The remaining figures describe that day's trading. They tell you the trading volume in $1,000 amounts; $48,000 of this specific issue traded that day. High, low, and closing prices are given, expressed as numerals that must be multiplied by 10 to get a dollar amount. Exxon 6½s traded at a high of 76⅝ or $766.25 and a low of 75⅞ or $758.75. The final trade of the day took place at 75⅞. There was a net change of −1⅛. That is, the closing price on this day was 1⅛ points ($11.25) lower than the closing price of the day before.

Yields

As prevailing interest rates rise or fall in response to economic conditions and government policy, the prices of bonds already in the market fluctuate above or below the face value. This keeps yields on these older issues competitive with those on new bonds. Investors would never buy an existing bond from another bondholder if they could get a higher return from a comparable new issue.

Current Yield When investors speak of a bond's yield they are generally referring to what is properly called its current yield. This figure is the quotient that results from dividing the amount of interest paid annually on a bond by its current price.

$$\frac{\text{annual interest}}{\text{current price}} = \text{current yield}$$

When a bond is bought at par, its current yield is identical to its coupon rate. At any other price, the current yield will be more or less than the coupon rate. We can use the data for the Exxon bond to see how this formula works. The annual interest rate is figured on the bond's face value (6½% or .065 × $1,000 = $65). This annual interest in dollars is divided by the current price ($65 ÷ $758.75) to get the current yield (.0856 or 8.6%). In the following example you can see how price changes affect the yield of a bond with a 9 percent coupon and a par value of $1,000.

Price	Yield
$1,000	9.0 %
1,100	8.18
900	10.0

Yield to Maturity Current yield is just one measure of a bond's return to investors. Even more important is a calculation called *yield to maturity*. This takes into account the potential capital gain or loss a person may realize by buying a bond for less or more than its par value. At par, a bond's yield to maturity is the same as its coupon rate or current yield. If a bond is bought at a discount, the yield to maturity is higher than current yield. If a bond is bought at a premium, the yield to maturity is less than current yield.

To determine yield to maturity, the compound annual interest gained or lost on the difference between a bond's current price and its par value must first be calculated. Part of this interest is then assigned to each year of the bond's remaining life. The result is expressed as a single annual percentage rate.

If that sounds complicated, it is. Bond traders usually use a computer to calculate yield to maturity. Using a bond value table is simpler, though less exact. Such tables give yield to maturity for various terms of maturity, coupon rates, and prices. Yields are expressed in whole percentages and smaller measurements known as *basis points*. One hundred basis points equal 1 percent. For example, a bond yield of 7.63 percent is 5 basis points lower than a 7.68 percent yield. A sample table from a bond value book is shown on page 20.

If you were thinking of buying the Exxon bond we have been discussing, you would first locate the 6½ percent coupon rate in the upper-left-hand corner. Next find the number that corresponds to the expected purchase price, the most recent closing price, in the column under the actual number of years left to maturity. In this case, let us assume that will be 10 years. The price, $758.75, falls between 75.09 and 76.11, which corresponds to yields of between 10.4 percent and 10.6 percent in the leftmost

6½% YEARS and MONTHS

YIELD	8-3	8-6	8-9	9-0	9-3	9-6	9-9	10-0	10-6	11-0	11-6	12-0
5.00	110.03	110.28	110.52	110.77	110.99	111.23	111.45	111.69	112.14	112.57	113.00	113.41
5.20	108.62	108.84	109.04	109.25	109.44	109.65	109.83	110.04	110.42	110.79	111.15	111.50
5.40	107.23	107.42	107.58	107.76	107.92	108.09	108.24	108.41	108.73	109.03	109.33	109.62
5.60	105.87	106.02	106.15	106.30	106.42	106.56	106.68	106.82	107.07	107.32	107.56	107.79
5.80	104.53	104.65	104.74	104.85	104.95	105.06	105.15	105.26	105.45	105.63	105.82	105.99
6.00	103.20	103.29	103.35	103.44	103.50	103.58	103.64	103.72	103.85	103.98	104.11	104.23
6.20	101.90	101.96	101.99	102.05	102.08	102.13	102.16	102.21	102.29	102.37	102.44	102.51
6.40	100.62	100.65	100.65	100.68	100.68	100.70	100.70	100.73	100.76	100.78	100.81	100.83
6.60	99.36	99.36	99.33	99.33	99.30	99.30	99.28	99.28	99.25	99.23	99.20	99.18
6.80	98.12	98.09	98.03	98.01	97.95	97.93	97.87	97.85	97.77	97.70	97.63	97.57
7.00	96.89	96.84	96.76	96.70	96.62	96.57	96.50	96.45	96.33	96.21	96.09	95.99
7.20	95.69	95.61	95.50	95.42	95.32	95.24	95.14	95.07	94.90	94.74	94.59	94.44
7.40	94.50	94.40	94.26	94.16	94.03	93.94	93.81	93.72	93.51	93.31	93.11	92.92
7.60	93.33	93.20	93.05	92.92	92.77	92.65	92.51	92.39	92.14	91.90	91.66	91.44
7.80	92.18	92.03	91.85	91.70	91.53	91.39	91.22	91.09	90.80	90.52	90.25	89.99
8.00	91.05	90.88	90.67	90.51	90.31	90.15	89.96	89.81	89.48	89.16	88.86	88.56
8.20	89.94	89.74	89.51	89.33	89.11	88.93	88.72	88.55	88.18	87.83	87.50	87.17
8.40	88.84	88.62	88.37	88.17	87.93	87.73	87.50	87.31	86.91	86.53	86.16	85.81
8.60	87.76	87.52	87.25	87.03	86.77	86.55	86.31	86.10	85.67	85.25	84.85	84.47
8.80	86.69	86.43	86.15	85.90	85.63	85.40	85.13	84.91	84.44	84.00	83.57	83.16
9.00	85.64	85.37	85.06	84.80	84.51	84.26	83.98	83.74	83.24	82.77	82.32	81.88
9.20	84.61	84.31	83.99	83.71	83.41	83.14	82.84	82.59	82.07	81.56	81.08	80.62
9.40	83.59	83.28	82.94	82.65	82.32	82.04	81.73	81.46	80.91	80.38	79.88	79.39
9.60	82.59	82.26	81.90	81.59	81.25	80.96	80.63	80.35	79.77	79.22	78.69	78.19
9.80	81.60	81.26	80.89	80.56	80.20	79.90	79.56	79.26	78.66	78.08	77.53	77.01
10.00	80.63	80.27	79.88	79.54	79.17	78.85	78.50	78.19	77.56	76.96	76.39	75.85
10.20	79.67	79.30	78.90	78.54	78.16	77.82	77.46	77.14	76.49	75.87	75.28	74.72
10.40	78.73	78.34	77.92	77.56	77.16	76.81	76.43	76.11	75.43	74.79	74.19	73.61
10.60	77.80	77.40	76.97	76.59	76.18	75.82	75.43	75.09	74.40	73.74	73.11	72.52
10.80	76.88	76.47	76.02	75.63	75.21	74.84	74.44	74.09	73.38	72.70	72.06	71.45
11.00	75.98	75.55	75.10	74.70	74.26	73.88	73.47	73.11	72.38	71.69	71.03	70.41
11.20	75.09	74.65	74.19	73.77	73.33	72.94	72.52	72.15	71.40	70.69	70.02	69.38
11.40	74.22	73.77	73.29	72.86	72.41	72.01	71.58	71.20	70.44	69.71	69.03	68.38
11.60	73.35	72.89	72.40	71.97	71.50	71.10	70.65	70.27	69.49	68.75	68.06	67.40
11.80	72.50	72.03	71.53	71.09	70.61	70.20	69.75	69.36	68.56	67.81	67.10	66.43
12.00	71.67	71.19	70.68	70.22	69.74	69.32	68.86	68.46	67.65	66.89	66.17	65.49
12.20	70.84	70.35	69.83	69.37	68.88	68.45	67.98	67.57	66.75	65.98	65.25	64.56
12.40	70.03	69.53	69.00	68.53	68.03	67.59	67.12	66.71	65.87	65.09	64.35	63.65
12.60	69.23	68.72	68.18	67.71	67.20	66.75	66.27	65.85	65.01	64.21	63.46	62.76
12.80	68.44	67.93	67.38	66.89	66.38	65.93	65.44	65.01	64.16	63.35	62.60	61.89
13.00	67.66	67.14	66.58	66.09	65.57	65.11	64.62	64.19	63.32	62.51	61.75	61.03
13.20	66.90	66.37	65.80	65.31	64.78	64.31	63.81	63.38	62.50	61.68	60.91	60.19
13.40	66.14	65.61	65.03	64.53	63.99	63.53	63.02	62.58	61.70	60.87	60.09	59.37
13.60	65.40	64.86	64.28	63.77	63.23	62.75	62.24	61.80	60.91	60.07	59.29	58.56
13.80	64.67	64.12	63.53	63.02	62.47	61.99	61.47	61.03	60.13	59.29	58.50	57.77
14.00	63.94	63.39	62.80	62.28	61.72	61.24	60.72	60.27	59.37	58.52	57.73	56.99
14.20	63.23	62.67	62.07	61.55	60.99	60.50	59.98	59.53	58.62	57.77	56.97	56.23
14.40	62.53	61.96	61.36	60.83	60.27	59.78	59.25	58.80	57.88	57.02	56.23	55.48
14.60	61.84	61.27	60.66	60.13	59.56	59.07	58.53	58.08	57.15	56.29	55.49	54.75
14.80	61.16	60.58	59.97	59.43	58.86	58.36	57.83	57.37	56.44	55.58	54.78	54.03
15.00	60.49	59.91	59.29	58.75	58.17	57.67	57.14	56.67	55.74	54.88	54.07	53.32
15.20	59.82	59.24	58.62	58.08	57.50	56.99	56.45	55.99	55.06	54.19	53.38	52.63
15.40	59.17	58.58	57.96	57.41	56.83	56.33	55.78	55.32	54.38	53.51	52.70	51.95
15.60	58.53	57.94	57.31	56.76	56.17	55.67	55.12	54.65	53.71	52.84	52.03	51.28
15.80	57.90	57.30	56.67	56.12	55.53	55.02	54.47	54.00	53.06	52.19	51.38	50.63
16.00	57.27	56.67	56.04	55.48	54.89	54.38	53.83	53.36	52.42	51.55	50.74	49.99
16.20	56.65	56.05	55.41	54.86	54.27	53.76	53.20	52.73	51.79	50.92	50.11	49.36
16.40	56.05	55.44	54.80	54.25	53.65	53.14	52.58	52.12	51.17	50.29	49.49	48.74
16.60	55.45	54.84	54.20	53.64	53.04	52.53	51.98	51.51	50.56	49.69	48.88	48.13
16.80	54.86	54.25	53.60	53.05	52.45	51.93	51.38	50.91	49.96	49.09	48.28	47.54
17.00	'28	53.67	53.02	52.46	51.86	51.34	50.79	50.32	49.37	8.50	47.69	46.95
17.20	'0	53.09	52.44	5'88	51.28	50.77	50.21	49.74	4ₚ	92	47.12	46.38
17.40		52.53	51.87		50.71	50.19	49.64	49.17		5	46.55	45.82
17.6ᐟ		51.97	5ᐟ		ᐟ5	49.63	49.07	48.6ᐟ			46.00	45.ᐟᐟ
17.		1.4ᐞ				ᐟ9.08	48.52	ᐟᐟ			45.ᐟ5	

Bond traders Jonathan Lake (left) and Larry Ansel, who trade previously issued bonds for the investment banking firm of Lebenthal & Co., work closely with bond dealers on behalf of their clients.

column. Because the Exxon bond is now priced at 75⅞, which is below face value on par, the yield to maturity is greater than the 8.6 percent current yield or the 6½ percent original rate.

Besides providing a more accurate picture of a buyer's potential return, figuring yields to maturity makes it possible to compare bonds of varying maturities and coupons. But yield to maturity is not necessarily the last word on the ultimate value of bonds. A bond may be called before reaching maturity, which reduces the number of years in which interest is paid and thus significantly lowers the yield.

When a Bond Is Called The issuers of most bonds can, if they wish, *call* in their bonds, or buy them back from

Some bonds may be redeemed before their maturity dates through the use of a sinking fund. This bond, issued in 1908 by the Cairo and Norfolk Railroad Company, contained a provision to establish a sinking fund of 2 percent of gross earnings of the company on May 1, 1913. The sinking fund could be used at that time or later.

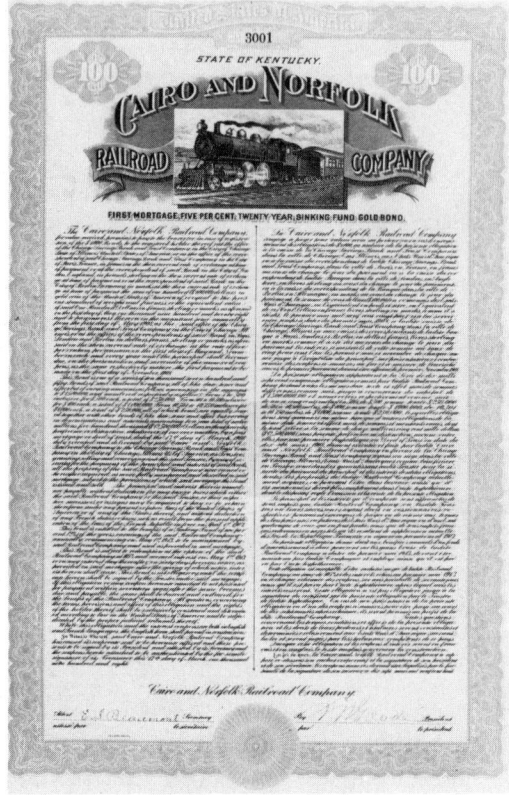

investors before the maturity date. Issuers generally call bonds early to take advantage of a drop in interest rates. For example, a corporation may sell a bond with a 10 percent coupon. Several years later interest rates for comparable issues fall to 8 percent. By calling in the 10 percent bonds and issuing new ones at 8 percent, the corporation can borrow the same amount of money and reduce its annual interest payments. The potential savings are often great enough that issuers are willing to pay a premium, or more than the bond's face value, to call in their bonds. The premium typically amounts to one year's interest.

A *call provision* on a bond must state the terms on which the bonds may later be called. Typically, a bond is safe from call for 5 or even 10 years after it first goes on the market. After that the issuer may redeem the bond at any time at a price stated on the bond's face.

Sinking Funds Bonds (and preferred stocks) may also be redeemed early through the use of a *sinking fund*, money set aside each year by the issuer for the purpose of redeeming securities periodically before their maturity dates. The securities to be redeemed each year can either be called at a specific price or purchased in the open market at prices set by the laws of supply and demand. Occasionally sinking fund payments are allowed to accumulate and earn interest over a longer period so an entire bond issue can be retired at one time. A sinking fund provision on the bond alerts investors to this possibility.

When bonds are called, investors get their principal back sooner but generally lose an attractive yield. Investors who bought bonds at a substantial premium may even lose part of their principal if the bond is called at a price close to par. For these reasons investors should carefully review call and sinking fund provisions with a broker or bond dealer before buying any fixed-income securities.

Ratings

Two major independent research companies, Standard & Poor's Corporation and Moody's Investors Service, rate the quality of bonds by estimating the probability that the issuer will meet the scheduled interest payments and return the principal at maturity. These two companies rate most publicly held corporate and municipal bonds. Moody's also rates many Treasury and agency issues. They do not rate privately placed bonds unless asked to do so, for a fee. Privately placed bonds are those bought directly from the

Securities analysts evaluate the potential of an industry's or a company's stocks or bonds. Here James Schainuck of Ladenburg, Thalmann & Co. examines a company report issued by one of the firms he follows.

issuer and not publicly distributed. In recent years nearly half of all bond issues have been private placements.

Both Standard & Poor's and Moody's use a simple system of letters to indicate their judgment of an issue's quality. Standard & Poor's ranks bonds using the first four letters of the alphabet in groups of three, as follows: AAA, AA, A; BBB, BB, B; and so on through D. Investors commonly refer to the highest rating as "Triple-A." Bonds rated D are in default, meaning that the issuer is unable to make scheduled interest payments. Moody's uses a similar system, but stops at C: Aaa, Aa, A; Baa, Ba, B; Caa, Ca, C. Some of the bonds in Moody's C category may be in default.

Other symbols can further refine a given rating. Standard & Poor's may add a plus or minus sign to a rating: an A+ is a shade higher than an A. Moody's uses A1 and Baa1 to indicate the highest quality municipal bonds.

In both systems rating groups from Triple-A through B carry the same meaning. Thus, Moody's opinion of an Aa bond is basically identical to Standard & Poor's judgment of an AA issue. Bonds rated below BBB or Baa are risky, not considered to be of investment quality or grade. Such bonds, known euphemistically as high-yield securities and pejoratively as junk bonds, typically pay several percentage points more in interest than less speculative issues. These ratings are published and available by subscription; you can usually find these publications at a local library or a brokerage office.

The rating agencies are extremely thorough and careful in researching their opinions. Each company employs a staff of securities analysts who examine an issuer's financial condition, operations, and management. Bond analysts also study documents such as the bond's *indenture,* which describes certain legal and technical details about the issue. Perhaps the most important factor is an evaluation of the company's future earnings potential or, in the case of municipal bonds, of a community's economic base. Ratings are constantly reviewed and sometimes changed to reflect improvement or deterioration in the issuer's overall financial condition.

U.S. Government Securities

The biggest borrower in the United States is the federal government, which supplements tax revenues by issuing four types of debt obligations. *Treasury bills* mature in 3, 6, or 12 months. *Treasury notes* come due in 1 to 10 years, while *bonds* mature in 10 to 30 years. Of all Treasury issues, *savings bonds,* which have a term of 12 years, are probably most familiar to individual investors. All but savings bonds are commonly known as Treasuries.

Treasury securities offer investors:
- Maximum safety of principal, because they are backed by the full faith and credit of the U.S. government. All are rated Triple-A.
- Competitive yields, although usually less than those of less secure corporate issues.
- Maximum call protection, with investors protected for at least 25 years.
- A high degree of liquidity, because they are actively traded in secondary markets.
- A tax break, because interest is exempt from state and local taxes.

The Treasury Department in Washington, D.C., issues the U.S. government's debt obligations.

Treasury Bills Commonly called T-bills, Treasury bills account for the bulk of government financing. The Treasury holds an auction for three- and six-month bills almost every week, and for one-year bills usually every month.

T-bills come in 5 denominations, from $10,000 to $100,000,000. The actual cost to an investor is generally lower. Competitive bids at the auction determine a bill's yield, which is usually higher than its coupon. But many investors buy bills at face value in noncompetitive bidding before the auction. To adjust the bill's yield, the Treasury refunds part of the purchase price to these investors. No interest is paid until the bill matures, when buyers receive the security's full par value. T-bills may not be called.

Treasury Notes You will need $5,000 to buy a treasury note that matures in less than 4 years but only $1,000 for one with a longer maturity. Notes have a fixed rate of interest, paid semiannually. Because of their longer maturities, notes typically offer higher yields than bills, but the risk of loss from rising rates is small. Notes may not be called.

Treasury Bonds Treasury bonds are securities that come in denominations as low as $1,000 and have a fixed interest rate. Unlike bills and notes, some Treasury bonds are call-

GOVERNMENT SECURITIES

able. But buyers are protected against call for much longer than investors in corporate or municipal securities. Only 30-year Treasuries are callable and then only after 25 years. Newspaper bond tables show the maturity date of such bonds in hyphenated form. For example, "1993–98" means that the bond matures in 1998 but can be called as early as 1993.

Buying Treasuries Bills, notes, or bonds can be bought at no commission directly from any of the 12 Federal Reserve Banks or their 25 branches. They can also be purchased by mail, by sending a certified personal check or cashier's check for the bill's face value to the Bureau of the Public Debt, Securities Transactions Branch, Washington, D.C. 20226. Some commercial banks, brokerage houses, and government securities dealers also sell Treasuries, at a commission of $25 to $50.

Agency Issues

Besides the Treasury, about 20 federal agencies sell notes and bonds to finance their operations. Known as Agencies, these securities have fixed coupon rates and maturity dates but are rarely callable.

Ginnie, Fannie, and Freddie The Government National Mortgage Association, a branch of the Department of Housing and Urban Development, is the largest issuer of Agency bonds. Its securities are known as Ginnie Maes (from the initials GNMA). Ginnie Maes, like Fannie Maes (issued by the Federal National Mortgage Association) and Freddie Macs (from the Federal Home Loan Mortgage Corporation), are available from brokers in $25,000 denominations.

Strictly speaking, Ginnies, Fannies, and Freddies are not bonds but *pass-through certificates*. The issuers use mortgages as collateral, and, as homeowners pay out mortgages, the issuing agencies pay out interest and a portion or principal in turn, passing the money through to investors every month. (Mortgages are loans made for the purchase of homes and other real estate. Collateral is property that belongs to a borrower and can be possessed by a lender if the borrower does not repay a loan on schedule. Collateral for a mortgage usually consists of the mortgaged property.)

Income from pass-throughs is less predictable than that from conventional bonds. The stated term on most certificates is 30 years, but when people sell or refinance their houses they retire the mortgage all at once, reducing the life of a pass-through to about 12 years on average. If interest rates go down, more homeowners prepay their mortgages, so investors receive a higher yield for a shorter time. As rates rise, there are fewer prepayments.

Because of their uncertain term and yield, pass-throughs earn at least one percentage point more in interest than Treasuries. Yet both have AAA ratings and some Agencies are backed by the federal government's full faith and credit.

CMOs Several years ago investment bankers created a new type of bond to take some of the uncertainty out of pass-throughs. Known as collateralized mortgage obligations or *CMOs*, these securities are backed by mortgages grouped according to whether their maturities are 5, 10, 20, or 30 years. Holders of CMOs receive regular interest payments, but repayments of principal accumulate until there is enough money to retire each group of bonds in order of maturity. CMOs can be bought from brokers in $1,000 denominations.

Savings Bonds Many of today's investors were first exposed to government bonds through the famous Series E Savings Bonds issued during World War II. Recent changes have made savings bonds a more attractive investment than in the past, when high inflation wiped out the value of the bonds' low fixed-interest rate.

In 1982 the Treasury changed to a variable interest rate on EE bonds, which replaced Es in 1980. Investors who hold 12-year EE bonds for 5 years or longer will receive 85 percent of the average yields paid on 5-year Treasury notes in the period in which they held the savings bonds. A 6 percent minimum return offers protection if interest rates drop, provided the bond is held for at least 5 years, but the interest rate can sink as low as 4 percent if the bond is redeemed earlier.

You can buy Series EE bonds at no commission from banks and payroll savings plans or by mail from the U.S. Treasury. The bonds come in denominations of $50 to $10,000, but you pay only half of the face value. As with T-bills, you do not receive interest payments but get the full value of the bond at maturity. You pay no state or local income tax on the interest and federal income tax is payable only in the year in which the bond matures or is redeemed.

Corporate Bonds

Bonds issued by corporations provide the highest current yields of any fixed-income securities. The interest from corporates, as these bonds are called, is fully taxable. For this reason they are often recommended for tax-deferred retirement accounts or for people in a low tax bracket. Corporates may also be a good buy for those in higher brackets, but their yields should be compared with those of municipals of comparable term and quality, which may be a better after-tax value. Some corporates are simply good investments for anyone.

Call provisions are particularly important for buyers of corporates. Issuers may call in their securities after only

Millions of people became bondholders during World War II. Celebrities often helped to sell the war bonds, which provided money to finance the war effort. Here prizefighter Jack Dempsey (left), a commander in the Coast Guard, accepts payment from a serviceman buying a bond for his daughter.

five years, which may leave the bondholders with money to reinvest at lower rates. To avoid this risk, buyers should look for bonds that were issued earlier, when interest rates were lower than at the time of purchase. Such *discount bonds* have yields that are competitive with those of new issues. But because the coupon rate is low, the issuer is less likely to redeem the bonds early. This gives the buyer time to follow the well-known adage, "Buy low, sell high."

A woman sells war savings stamps in World War II. Buyers pasted their stamps in a booklet; when filled with $18.75 worth of stamps, it was exchanged for a $25 savings bond.

Empire State Plaza in Albany, New York, was built with the proceeds from the sale of bonds issued by the state.

Municipal Bonds

Municipal bonds, also called munis or tax-exempts, are issued by states, cities, towns, or their authorities (such as housing or bridge and tunnel authorities). Tax-exempts usually finance construction of new highways, hospitals, sewage disposal plants, sports stadiums, and other public projects.

Municipals differ from corporate bonds in several ways. First and most important, interest on municipals is exempt from federal income taxes. Investors who live in the state of issue are usually exempt from state and local taxes as well.

Second, municipals typically have serial maturities, meaning that a portion of the total issue matures each year until the entire issue has been retired. Unlike sinking fund retirements, each year in a serial issue has its own interest rate or is priced to provide a specific yield. Several years ago, for example, the state of Maryland issued $145 million of 15-year Triple-A bonds at a 4.86 percent yield. The bonds were reoffered to investors on the following *partial scale*, as such a series of yields is known: 1977 priced to yield 3.7 percent, 1980 to yield 3.9 percent, 1981 to yield 4.1 percent, and so on, ending with a 5.2 percent yield in 1991.

Third, most municipals are issued in $5,000 denominations, compared with $1,000 on most Treasuries and corporates. Finally, whereas corporate bonds are often listed on the New York or American Stock Exchanges, municipal bonds trade entirely in the over-the-counter market. This means that muni prices are usually not quoted in the financial pages of daily newspapers. An investor interested in a specific issue must consult a bond dealer for a price. Dealers themselves frequently consult the *Blue List of Current Municipal Offerings*, a daily publication of Standard & Poor's, which gives information such as price and yield on available offerings.

GOs vs. Revenue Bonds The most common type of tax-exempt is the *general obligation bond*. The governments that issue GOs promise to use their taxing power to insure that principal and interest payments are made on time. *Revenue bonds*, by contrast, are backed only by the earning power of the facility being built with the bond's proceeds. General obligation bonds typically are safer and have lower yields than comparable revenue bonds, since taxes are a more predictable source of funds than, say, the income from a toll road. GOs, therefore, usually have higher ratings than the revenue issues. Insured tax-exempts are available for those investors who are worried about an issuer's ability to meet payments. Private companies agree to pay the bond's interest and principal if the

A construction worker inspects the interior of a sewer-pipe section at a road-building site in California. The building of roads is one of many types of projects funded by government bonds.

seller defaults. Such insurance automatically raises a bond's rating to Triple-A.

Figuring Yields on Munis   Because interest on munis is tax-exempt, the coupons on such bonds tend to be several percentage points lower than on corporates, or even on Treasuries, which are subject to federal tax. Depending on the investor's tax bracket, a tax-exempt issue may result in a greater net gain. For example, an investor in the 28 percent bracket (as set up by the Tax Reform Act of 1986) would need a corporate yielding about 9.7 percent to equal the tax-exempt yield from a 7 percent municipal bond. Because tax laws change, and investors' incomes also change, it's important to estimate the tax consequences of any investment. Many people consult accountants before deciding whether to buy tax-exempts or corporate bonds.

Convertible Bonds

Convertibles, or converts, are issued by corporations. Like other bonds, they have a par value, coupon rate, maturity date, yield, and often a rating and a call date. If the issuer goes into bankruptcy, investors in other types of bonds from the issuer may have a prior claim on assets. But that is not the major difference between convertibles and so-called straight bonds.

What sets convertibles apart is that the investor is able to exchange the bonds for (convert them into) shares of the issuer's common stock. Interest on convertibles is lower than that on the same issuer's straight bonds but higher than the dividend yield on the issuer's common stock. This extra yield protects convertible prices from falling as fast as stock prices. At the same time, investors get a chance to share in the company's good fortune if its stock price soars. Prices of converts rise more slowly than those of stocks but faster than those of mortgage bonds. In short, convertible buyers give up some safety and interest in exchange for higher potential profits.

This five percent convertible bond can be exchanged for shares of Farah Manufacturing Company's common stock.

To companies raising money, convertibles have an advantage because they carry lower coupon rates than ordinary bonds. Companies also benefit from tax savings when they issue convertibles because interest payments on convertibles and other bonds can be deducted from a company's taxable income, whereas cash dividends paid on common stock come out of after-tax earnings. This is a short-term benefit, of course, that lasts only until the bonds are converted to common stock.

Judging Convertibles For investors, convertibles offer much of the safety of bonds plus the capital gain potential of common stock. But the dual nature of converts makes them one of the most complicated securities to use effectively. Investors must first decide whether they want to own the underlying stock they would get by converting the bond. An investor who does not want that stock should not buy that bond.

The next step is to calculate how long it will be before the convertible's higher yield compensates for its premium over the common stock price. Suppose you are considering a convertible, $1,000 face value, that pays 9 percent and has a conversion price of $25. This means that it may be exchanged for 40 shares of common stock at $25 a share. The stock now sells at $20 a share. With the bond priced at par, or $1,000, you are paying a 20 percent premium, $200 more than 40 shares of stock are worth in the market. Assuming the stock's dividend yield is 4 percent, or 80 cents a share, you would receive $32 a year if you bought 40 shares. By contrast, the 9 percent convertible gives you $90, or $58 more in annual income. It will take about 3½ years ($200 divided by $58) to reach what convertible traders call "breakeven." To be attractive, converts generally must reach breakeven in four years or less.

The time it takes for a convertible to break even is just one of the variables that investors should consider before buying. They can further limit their risk by selecting converts that have the following characteristics:

- A yield close to that on the company's straight bonds.
- A conversion price close to the common stock's current price.
- Underlying shares on which substantial appreciation is expected.

GETTING STARTED IN BONDS

You can buy or sell small quantities of bonds through a broker or a bond dealer, but commissions on such transactions can cut sharply into your net yield. It is usually easier to get into bonds by means of such pooled investments as a mutual fund or a unit trust. For a minimum initial investment of $1,000 you can share in a diversified portfolio of securities worth millions of dollars. You can choose to receive interest payments monthly or have them reinvested automatically. A fund or trust is the only way for small investors to own Ginnie Maes, which are sold in $25,000 denominations, or to invest safely in high-yielding but low-rated issues. Funds and trusts are also a practical approach to buying municipal bonds, which are issued in $5,000 denominations.

Many funds are available through brokers, who generally charge an 8 percent sales commission. Brokers also sell units in trusts for a fee of about 5 percent. You can buy no-load bond mutual funds, at no sales charge, directly from an investment company.

Unit trusts are similar in some ways to bond mutual funds and indeed often refer to themselves as funds. How-

Gail S. Dickstein, a bond dealer for Lebenthal & Co., advises investors on their holdings and handles transactions for them.

ever, mutual funds constantly buy and sell bonds, while the trusts have a fixed portfolio. Because a trust holds all securities until they reach maturity, it can guarantee to return your principal in full. The return from interest may be lower than from a mutual fund, but you cannot receive less than you paid when you redeem your shares in a trust. In a bond fund, on the other hand, you may lose part of your principal if you sell your shares when bond prices are down.

PREFERRED STOCKS

Preferred stocks are much like bonds, except that they do not have a maturity date and they represent part ownership in a company and not a loan. Like bonds, preferreds offer relatively attractive yields. They can be called, some can be converted into common stock, some are rated, most are issued at a stated par value (usually $100), and all are listed as senior securities. Indeed, some preferred stocks are of such high quality that their market prices parallel those of top-rated long-term bonds.

Preferred stocks are a safer investment than the common stocks of the same issuer. This is because if a company is dissolved, the holders of its preferred stocks have preference over common stockholders when creditors are paid. Preferred stockholders also have a prior claim in the payment of dividends. Preferred stocks have ratings that appear identical to bond ratings. Their ratings, however, are not directly comparable because bonds are debt obligations and preferred stocks represent equity (ownership).

Although the dividend on preferred stock is set at a fixed annual rate, the issuer can change it at any time and even omit it entirely. For this reason most investors look for *cumulative preferred* stock. With this type of security, dividends that are skipped or "passed" (a decision made by the company's board of directors) are allowed to accumulate and must eventually be paid out. *Participating preferred* stocks enable the investor to share in any extra dividend payments that may be declared by the issuer for common shareholders. Most preferreds are nonparticipating, however, with income limited to the fixed annual dividend payment.

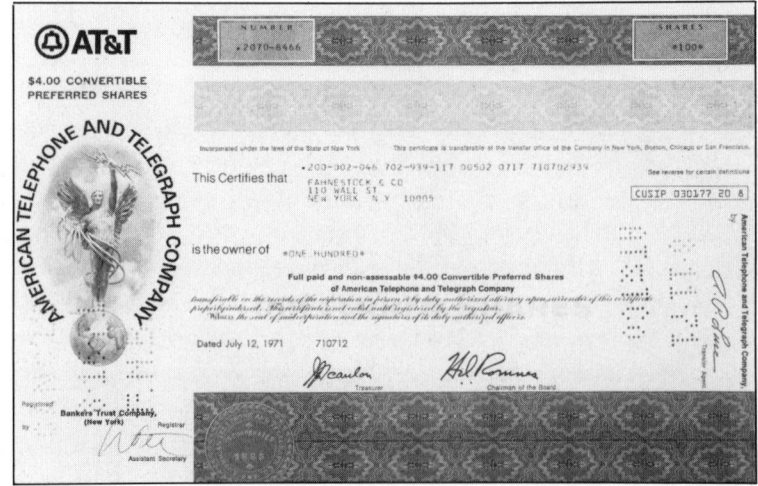

Certificate for 100 shares of preferred stock in American Telephone and Telegraph Company. The shareholder has the option of converting these shares into AT&T's common stock.

Shareholders attend an annual meeting of the Exxon Corporation. Holders of common stock have voting rights, but holders of preferred generally do not.

Holders of preferred stock have prior claims over common stockholders when it comes to dividends and company assets. However, their investment is still an equity, or ownership, interest. Bondholders, on the other hand, have invested in the debt obligations of companies. They thus have legally enforceable claims against an issuer who defaults on interest payments. Holders of preferred stock do not have legally protected claims against an issuer who does not pay a dividend.

Corporations have generally favored bonds over preferred stocks when they need to raise new capital. Bond interest is paid from earnings before taxes whereas preferred dividends are paid from after-tax earnings. Thus, preferred stocks can be more expensive to the corporation.

A preferred stock has some characteristics of a bond and some of common stock. It can offer the higher yield of a bond and has priority over the common stock in equity ownership, but it does not have the safety of a bond and its participation in the company's growth is limited. When buying preferreds, investors should strive for high income with the greatest possible safety. This is possible, for example, with a preferred from a company with few other preferred issues. Investors should also look for high income with growth possibilities, such as a preferred that is con-

Common stocks, such as those pictured here, have a lower claim on a company's dividends and assets than do preferred stocks.

vertible into common stock. Otherwise it is probably better to own straight or convertible bonds or the common stock of the company.

THE MONEY MARKET

Most bonds and stocks attract investors who want their money to earn some money over a long period of time. But many investors, including corporations, banks, and municipal governments, as well as individuals, do not want to lock their money away for 30 or 10 years, or even 1 year. The money market, in which surplus funds can be invested as briefly as overnight, is the ideal solution. It also serves borrowers who need to raise cash quickly for short-term use.

The money market consists of short-term credit instruments. Each type of credit offering is in effect a market in and of itself. Short-term credit instruments include Treasury bills, commercial paper (the IOUs, or debt notes, of corporations), negotiable certificates of deposit (CDs), bankers' acceptances (a type of loan), and commercial bank borrowings. Except for the bank borrowings, these transactions all create "negotiable paper." These are promissory notes pledging the return of the investors' principal at maturity and fixed interest payments in the meantime. These promissory notes are themselves marketable, which means they can be bought and sold.

All money market transactions mature within one year, and most have maturities of 90 days or less. The money market offers three main advantages over other sources of fixed-income investments. First, it is a large and liquid market, capable of handling billions of dollars with only slight effects on yields and able to make payments when needed.

Second, it offers a high degree of safety because issuers generally have good credit ratings. Investors should realize, however, that certain credit instruments can never be completely free of risk. When the Penn Central Railroad went bankrupt in 1970, for example, it had $82 million in commercial paper—debt notes—outstanding.

Third, most money market maturities are short term, coming due within 90 days. There is minimal risk of loss because interest rates are not likely to change greatly in such a brief period.

Components of the Money Market   By far the most influential participant in the money market is the Federal Reserve System. Through the Open Market Trading Desk at the New York Federal Reserve Bank, the Fed implements the decisions of its Open Market Committee. By selling and buying Treasury bills and other money market instruments, the Fed contracts or expands the reserve positions of some 6,000 commercial banks that are members of the system. In this way the Federal Reserve helps to shape monetary and credit conditions throughout the country.

The interest rates of bank certificates of deposit, which usually are higher than rates on Treasury bills with the same comparable maturity dates, are displayed in banks to attract investor interest.

Commercial banks are other important participants in the money market. They lend money to each other at the federal funds rate or borrow from Federal Reserve banks at the discount rate. Certificates of deposit or CDs are receipts that banks issue for money deposited for a fixed period of time. Commercial paper, or short-term promissory notes, are given to lenders by borrowing businesses. Because the interest rates on commercial paper are traditionally lower than on bank loans, such paper is frequently used to raise money for business operations. Other short-term debt notes, such as tax anticipation bills, bankers' acceptances, and repurchase agreements with government securities dealers, are also bought and sold in the money market.

Each type of money market instrument constitutes a separate market. Treasury bills trade in one large, nationwide market, certificates of deposit in another, and commercial paper in a third. Each market sets its own interest rates, but all rates tend to move closely together. Rates on most money market instruments are generally higher than that of the T-bill rate on comparable maturities, in order to attract investors away from the extremely safe government security.

The Money Market and You Small investors commonly participate in the money market by buying a CD, opening a bank money market account, or buying shares in either a taxable or tax-exempt money market mutual fund. Issued by a bank, a CD locks in an interest rate for as little as a week and as long as five years. Interest rates are higher for longer-term certificates. But you lose up to three months' interest if you cash in your certificate before it matures.

Bank money market accounts and mutual funds let you share in a pool of short-term debt obligations, many of which pay higher interest than you can get with a CD. Banks will guarantee their money market account rate for a month, but the yield of funds changes daily. Some banks and funds let you write checks on your money market investments.

Whether you choose a bank account, mutual fund, or CD, you can get your principal back in full when you want it, either immediately or after a brief waiting period. Certificates of deposit and bank money market accounts have federal deposit insurance to back up this promise, but money market mutual funds are almost as safe. Money market instruments, like bonds and preferred stocks, can be for many investors either an effective complement or a valuable alternative to common stocks.

GLOSSARY

basis point Unit used in expressing bond yields; one basis point equals .01 percentage point.

bearer bonds Bonds issued before July 1983 whose owners' names do not have to be registered with the issuing organization. Any person possessing a bearer bond may receive payments of interest and principal due on that bond.

bond A certificate that represents a loan to a company, government, or government agency. The issuing organization or company (the borrower) pays interest for the use of the money and must repay the face value of the bond at maturity.

call The repurchase of an issue of bonds or preferred stocks by the issuer prior to the maturity date.

certificate of deposit (CD) A bank receipt for money left to earn interest at a specific rate for a fixed period of time.

collateral Valuable property belonging to a borrower and used as security for a loan. In the event of default, it is forfeited to the lender.

CMO Acronym for Collateralized Mortgage Obligation; a bond backed by a collection of mortgages that are guaranteed by a mortgage association of the federal government.

convertible securities Corporate bonds or preferred stock that may be exchanged for the common stock of the issuing firm.

coupon rate The set interest rate on a bond.

current yield The amount of interest, expressed as a percent, that a bond is currently earning; determined by dividing the annual yield by current price.

discount The amount below face value at which a bond or preferred stock sells.

discount rate The interest rate paid by member banks of the Federal Reserve System on funds borrowed from the Federal Reserve Bank.

dividend A portion of a company's earnings that is distributed to stockholders; the amount is determined by the board of directors.

Fannie Maes Securities issued by the Federal National Mortgage Corporation and backed by a collection of mortgages.

federal funds rate The interest rate paid by a member bank of the Federal Reserve System when it borrows from another member bank.

Federal Reserve System The central banking system of the United States, which supervises the nation's banking system and sets appropriate monetary policy.

floating rate bonds Bonds whose rates are adjusted periodically by the issuer in order to reflect prevailing interest rates.

Freddie Macs Securities issued by the Federal Home Loan Mortgage Corporation and backed by a collection of mortgages.

general obligation bonds Municipal bonds backed by tax revenues to insure that principal and interest payments are made on time.

Ginnie Maes Securities issued by the Government National Mortgage Association and backed by a collection of mortgages.

indenture A written statement describing the legal and technical details of a bond's issue.

inflation A rise in prices that causes money to lose purchasing power and interest rates to increase.

interest rate The payment, usually a fixed percentage of the amount borrowed, that a lender receives for the use of money.

maturity date The date on which the issuer

of a bond must repay the principal to the lender.

money market The short-term credit market in which a variety of IOUs, bank notes, and treasury bills are traded. These instruments typically pay high rates of interest and preserve the value of the invested capital.

money market rate Percent of interest paid at a given time on money market instruments; largely determined by the yield of three-month Treasury bills.

mutual fund An investment in which the money of many investors is combined and invested in a wide range of securities.

obligations Government and corporate bonds.

par value or *face value* The value of a stock or bond that appears on the certificate.

pass-through certificates Securities (such as Ginnie Maes) that use mortgages as collateral and pay out a portion of interest and principal to investors each month as mortgage payments are made.

portfolio The securities held by an individual or institution.

preferred stock Stock that has a priority claim over common stock on assets, dividends, and earnings of a company.

premium The amount above face value at which a bond or preferred stock sells.

prime rate The interest rate that commercial banks charge their most creditworthy customers, such as major corporations.

principal The amount of money actually invested or borrowed.

put bonds Bonds that can be sold back to the issuer on a specified date or dates.

revenue bonds Municipal bonds that are payable from revenues earned by the facilities being built with the bonds' proceeds.

savings bonds U.S. Treasury securities with a term of 12 years.

senior securities Bonds and preferred stocks that have higher claims to an issuer's assets than other securities.

share of stock Any of the equal parts into which the entire value, or equity, of a company is divided. It represents part ownership in the company.

sinking fund Money set aside by an issuing company for the purpose of redeeming securities before their maturity date.

stock exchange A market, such as the New York Stock Exchange, in which securities are sold at prices determined by supply and demand.

term The period of time from the issue date to the maturity date of bonds and other investment loans.

Treasury bills Short-term U.S. Treasury securities, the interest on which is paid at maturity.

Treasury notes U.S. Treasury securities with terms of 1 to 10 years and fixed rates of interest, paid semiannually.

unit trust fund An investment in which the money of many investors is combined and invested in a portfolio of bonds held to their maturity dates.

yield to maturity A bond's total return to an investor from the time it is bought until its maturity date. If a bond is bought at a discount, the yield to maturity is greater than the current yield. If a bond is bought at a premium, the yield to maturity is less than current yield.

zero-coupon bonds Bonds sold at a discount from their face value and that pay no interest until they are redeemed.

FURTHER READING

Andrew, John. *Buying Municipal Bonds*. New York: Free Press, 1987. Emphasizes the municipal bond market after the Tax Reform Act of 1986.

Buying Treasury Securities at Federal Reserve Banks. A booklet that explains how to buy treasuries is available for $2 from the Federal Reserve Bank of Richmond, Public Services Department, Box 27622, Richmond, VA 23261.

Darst, David. *The Handbook of the Bond and Money Markets*. New York: McGraw-Hill, 1981. A definitive analysis of all types of fixed income securities.

Money, published by Time, Inc. The "Fundwatch" column in this monthly magazine surveys the top-performing money-market, bond, and stock mutual funds.

INDEX

Agencies, 27–29

Bankers' acceptances, 41, 42
Banks, commercial, in money market, 41, 42, 43
Basis points, 19
Bearer bonds, 13
Blue List of Current Municipal Offerings, 32
Bond(s). *See also* Government securities
 call provisions, 22–23, 29–30
 convertible, 34–36
 defined, 11–14
 funds and trusts, 36–37
 municipal, 31–33
 myths about, 10–11
 vs. preferred stock, 39
 ratings, 23–25
 sinking fund provisions, 23
 yields, 18–21
Bond prices
 and interest rates, 14, 18
 quotations, 16–18
Brokers, 36

Call provisions, 22–23, 29–30

Certificates of deposit (CDs), 40, 42, 43
Collateral, 12, 27, 28
Collateralized mortgage obligations (CMOs), 28
Commercial paper, 40, 42
Common stock, 9, 11, 13, 37
 convertibles, 34, 35
Convertible bonds, 34–36
Corporate bonds, 29–30
Coupon, 12–13
Coupon rate, 18, 19
Cumulative preferred stock, 38
Current yield, 18

Discount, 16
Discount bonds, 30
Discount rate, 15, 42

Face value, 12, 16
Fannie Maes, 27
Federal fund rate, 15, 42
Federal Home Loan Mortgage Corporation, 27
Federal National Mortgage Association (FNMA), 27
Federal Reserve Banks, 15, 27, 42

Federal Reserve Board, 15
Federal Reserve System, 15, 41
Floating-rate bonds, 13
Freddie Macs, 27

General obligation bonds (GOs), 32–33
Ginnie Maes, 27, 36
Government National Mortgage Association (GNMA), 27, 36
Government securities, 12, 15, 17
  agencies, 27–29
  treasuries, 25–27, 40, 41

High-yield securities, 25

Indenture, 25
Inflation, 15
Interest, compound annual, 19
Interest rates, 42
  and bond prices, 14, 18
  influences on, 14–15
  interrelationship of, 15–16
  variable, 29

Junk bonds, 25

Maturity
  date, 12, 15
  serial, 31–32
  yield to, 19–20
Money market, 11, 40–43
Money market rates, 16, 42–43
Moody's Investors Service, 23, 24
Mortgages, 27–28
Municipal bonds, 31–33
Mutual funds, 36–37, 43

Negotiable paper, 41

Obligations, 12
Open Market Committee, 41

Partial scale, 32

Participating preferred stock, 38
Par value, 12, 16, 19, 37
Pass-through certificates, 27–28
Preferred stock, 13–14, 37–40
Premium, 16
Prime rate, 16
Principal, 12
Put bonds, 13

Quotations, price, 16–18

Ratings
  bond, 23–25
  preferred stock, 38

Savings bonds, 25, 28–29
Serial maturities, 31–32
Short-term credit instruments, 40–41, 42, 43
Sinking fund provisions, 23
Standard & Poor's Corporation, 23, 24, 32
Stock. *See* Common stock; Preferred stock

Tax deductions, convertibles, 35
Tax exemptions, municipals, 31, 32, 33
Term, 12, 15
Treasuries, 25–27, 40, 41
Treasury, U.S., 25, 26, 27, 29
Treasury bills (T-bills), 16, 25, 26, 40, 41
Treasury bonds, 26–27
Treasury notes, 25, 26
Triple-A rating, 24

Unit trust, 36–37

Wall Street Journal, 17

Yield
  on convertibles, 34
  on corporate bonds, 29
  current, 18
  to maturity, 19–20
  on municipals, 33

Zero-coupon bonds, 13

JEFFREY B. LITTLE, a finance graduate of New York University, began his Wall Street career in the early 1960s. He has worked as an accountant for a retail brokerage firm, as an instructor of technical analysis in a broker training center, as a securities analyst of technology stocks, and as a portfolio manager and advisory committee member for a major mutual fund. He is a Fellow of the Financial Analysts Federation, a member of the New York Society of Security Analysts, and was formerly a vice-president of an investment counsel firm in Baltimore.

PAUL A. SAMUELSON, senior editorial consultant, is Institute Professor Emeritus at the Massachusetts Institute of Technology. He is author (now coauthor) of the best-selling textbook *Economics*. He served as an adviser to President John F. Kennedy and in 1970 was the first American to win the Nobel Prize in economics.

SHAWN PATRICK BURKE, consulting editor, is a securities analyst with Standard & Poor's Corporation. He has been an internal consultant in industry as well as for a Wall Street investment firm, and he has extensive experience in computer-generated financial modeling and analysis.

PAT DREYFUS, contributing editor, is a free-lance writer based in New York City who specializes in financial and investment topics. She has been a staff writer for *Forbes* and *Money* magazines and is a graduate of Wellesley College.

PICTURE CREDITS AP/Wide World Photos: p. 14; The Bettmann Archive: pp. 29, 30; Paul Duckworth/Photoreporters: p. 26; courtesy of Exxon: p. 39; Mark Ferri: pp. 21, 24, 37; reproduced from Pub. No. 183, Bond Values Tables, copyright 1981, p. 252, Financial Publishing Company, Boston, MA 02215: p. 20; Charles Marden Fitch/Taurus Photos: p. 40; George Haling: cover; Ellis Herwig/Taurus Photos: p. 33; Betsy Levin: pp. 8, 42; Rafael Macia/Photo Researchers: p. 34; R.M. Smythe & Co., Inc.: pp. 12, 22, 38; Russell A. Thompson/Taurus Photos: p. 31; *Wall Street Journal*: p. 17; Shirley Zeiberg/Taurus Photos: p. 10.

WITHDRAWN
Emmaus High School Library
Emmaus, Pennsylvania

332.63　　　　　　　　　　B4043
LIT　　　Little, Jeffrey B.
　　　　　　Bonds, preferred
　　　　　stocks, and the

TITLE

4043

332.63　　　　　　　　　　B4043
LIT　　　Little, Jeffrey B.
　　　　　　Bonds, preferred
　　　　　stocks, and the